Currents in the Stream

Currents in the Stream

Poems by

Charlotte Cox

NORTH STAR PRESS OF ST. CLOUD, INC.

St. Cloud, Minnesota

ISBN: 978-0-87839-783-9

Printed in the United States of America

First edition: September 2014

Published by
North Star Press of St. Cloud, Inc.
P.O. Box 451
St. Cloud, MN 56302

www.northstarpress.com

To
Larry,
who, for better or for worse,
inspired many of these poems

To
Anna, Emma, Caleb, Lucy, and Jack,
who I hope might read some of them
to their own grandchildren

Table of Contents

I.
Midwest Moorings

II.
Nature's Flow

III.
Family Gatherings

IV.
On the Move

V.
Between Two Worlds

VI.
Coming Home Alone

I.

Midwest Moorings

Inside the Egg

The sealed boat cover
on this first day of spring
is a bright shroud of blue shrink-wrap.
As I struggle to pry up the edges,
I put my head inside a moment,
then catch my breath to glimpse
a screen of glowing shadows,
another kind of world.

Clear silhouettes of leaves
and branches hover just beyond
translucent plastic. This must be how
a hatching chick feels before it starts
to peck apart its fragile shell,
still encased in dreaming safety
but eager to use that sharp eggtooth,
to see what's out there and get to it.

Or how a child lying on the grass,
looking up into a clear dark sky,
suspended in the cup of night,
sheltered by the breath of earth,
thrills to the glittering dance of stars,
planets, asteroids, that flicker, spinning
through their own boundless worlds,
and reaches out to touch their splendor.

So we yearn. With each new layer, we vow
to tear the membrane, crack the shell,
grasp in full the next new world
where life awaits. And we know,
every time, deep inside,
that it's only the beginning.

The Truth About Birds

One day when I was four, I tiptoed down the basement stairs,
toward a circle of three men squatting in the damp, dim light—
my teasing father and his younger, raucous brothers, calling,
laughing, "Come on, come on, see the Christmas surprise."

They held something lumpy, moving, covered in a gunnysack—
when a sudden storm of goose exploded from the rough cloth,
wings beating, feet flying, me crying. It was months
before I could look at a pillow feather on the floor.

Another year when my father lost his job and I was six,
we stayed at my great-grandma's farm. Hard times, cold beds.
I saw how chickens were killed (another arena, different men)
in the yard behind the house. "Watch this," they roared,

and laid the unsuspecting bird's head on the old tree stump.
Then whack! The flashing axe came down. The head lay lifeless
on the flat gray stump, red eyes still glaring, while the body
fluffed and flapped around the grass forever on mindless legs.

At eight, I kept a crippled canary who'd warble in the sunlight
but could not cling to perch with his knotty twisted feet, so
we'd leave his cage door open and he'd grip the wire-edge there,
falling off at times, then picked up again and set to rights.

Except the night we forgot him. When he tumbled to the carpet,
in the dark he waited, until my father's bare foot found him
on a pre-dawn bathroom trip—"What the hell?"—flattening
his yellow body and tiny bones with a cry to pierce the heart.

So in midlife, eight months pregnant, when my gentle first-born
daughter toddles up to me, holding out her present
in a napkin, while my earnest mate says, "Go on, show Mommy
what you found outside," I know too well what it will be—

a tiny, featherless creature, unopened eyes bulging softly,
scrawny neck askew, heart meant for 200 beats a minute—
now still. Feeling my stomach turn, eyes burn, heart wrench,
I close her napkin gently and say, "Take it back to Daddy, dear."

My fertile womb and tender brain rebel: No more feathers,
no more killing, no more left for dead. Instead I vow
to nurture the unfolding embryo within me and be sure
that it emerges growing strong, pushing for dear life.

Learning to Play Ball

On days like this, cool air, warm sun, it's easy to go
back in time, to long-lost childhood freedoms—loose rules,
vacant lots, open-ended days. ("Be home before dark,"
mothers shouted as we skipped out the door.)
Back then there was always a gang of neighbor kids
looking for a softball game after school.

Now, when I pass a certain kind of empty field,
where dusty paths outline a diamond and sandbag bases
are left out from day to day, it all comes back—
I'm eight again, I can smell the leather of my glove,
feel the heft of a beat-up softball in my hand,
sense my pulse rise, anticipating the first pitch.

The littlest kids played outfield in those days. Why?
Because out there you'd do the least amount of damage.
So you'd stand there, inning after inning, in the tall grass,
waiting, waiting, dying for the chance to make a play,
dreading that miracle moment when a high fly ball
would really come to you. (Oh no, it's me, at last!)

Later, at bat, you'd try to pick up moves—flexing knees,
kicking dirt, coiling shoulder muscles, tapping the plate.
"Just meet the ball," your side would yell, "don't try to blast it,"
but the other side would taunt, "Hey, batta-batta, swing!" And
once in a while, when the ball met the sweet spot on your bat,
the resounding crack would be the best thing you'd ever felt.

Who cares today? We never got a trophy or played leagues.
The thrill was in the possibilities—every game was new.
We didn't even know we were learning things that would
last us all our lives: Keep your eye on the ball. Be patient,
but be ready. Back up your teammates. Never give up,
the tide can turn. You can't win 'em all. Your time will come.

Empty Houses, Waiting to Be Filled

We tiptoed through soft sawdust, leftover tools and tarps,
detoured around the open gaps of unbuilt stairwells,
saw the sandwich crusts dropped by careless workers,
kicked an empty green Coke bottle near the doorframe.

We used that prop to start a game of spin-the-bottle,
daring ourselves, still half-bewildered kids, eleven or twelve,
to form a ragged circle in a cleaned-up corner space,
bare joists showing the rooms beyond in late-day sunlight.

It was less lust than contest: who gets chosen, who looks good
with whom, who can press lips tightest, hold breath longest—
the girls gasping and appalled yet jittering to go again,
the boys concerned (for once) with furthering an education:

Lip-feel, hands-place, stand-or-sit, wet-or-dry (no question
yet of tongues). We even got excited by the watching—
spectators as well as players in this brand-new age-old game—
who can stand it, who can take it, who's the fairest of us all?

The Way Out

He picked up the gun, just a .22,
hefted it in his hands, felt the weight,
as cool gray daylight glinted on the barrel.
He knew well the report that it would make
from all the times, by age fourteen, he'd used it
on tin cans on a fence, or garden rabbits,
or those squirrels he'd hunted in the woods,
knew there would be blood, a ragged hole.

There might be pain, not much, his aim was sure.
But was anything else? What would come next?
He knew there must be more than this. He knew
from books it could be a river with a boatman,
or from stories it could be another lifetime,
or from church there'd be a sacred tunnel,
a passageway, with light and glory at the end.
Yes, a way out of all this growing emptiness.

He knew too much, had learned too fast—
the early tricks, IQ tests, gifted ed,
accelerating him at a breakneck pace
his mind craved but heart could not sustain.
It was a carnival ride, such fun at first,
that spun him faster, faster, and finally
swept him up toward a windy pinnacle,
alone, where no one else could touch him.

No triumph, just a sense of finishing the race
in silence. He'd lived out his life, condensed
it all. Yet what remained was never-ending
curiosity—what would this last hurdle

be like? Nobody alive knew that, and those
who'd crossed the line could send no message back.
Yet all seemed right, take the next step—he could
be first again, and grasp that last enigma.

Surely those predicting nothingness were wrong.
What would be the point? Just an abrupt ending?
Like those old-time movies where the last images
flickered on the screen while the loose film-end
popped off the reel and continued flapping in
the darkness? He laid a cartridge in the chamber
and slid the bolt home. No one came to mind
who'd mind—his parents still would have each other.

He placed the gun upright between his feet,
and leaned his forehead forward on the barrel.
All he could think of was release, stillness,
and maybe some new place with others like him.
He squeezed his eyes shut tight. As he pressed down
hard on the trigger, a few last images flashed
behind his eyelids, and he thought he heard
the sound of film-end spinning off the reel.

Synergy

Tiny yellow crop duster—

flitting upwards

toward the blue

at an angle,

wings slanted sharp,

wheeling in wild abandon,

then diving deep and

skimming corn tassels,

a butterfly with a purpose,

flirting with gravity,

shooting so low that

a tall man could sting

his upstretched hands

on the unretractable wheels,

finishing one row precisely,

then bursting up again

in freeform arcs,

a crazy synergy

of spontaneous grace

and steely-eyed control,

above any issues of

preservation or pollution—

you create unplanned beauty

from pure energy.

Midwest Highways

It's a blazing blue, cloud-puffed July day in the heartland—
primetime summertime in this part of the rolling green prairies—
and I'm busy cranking out the familiar miles home
from a so-so day, down the well-trodden ruts of the interstate,
when they roar up on the right, then swerve left,
like an apparition from the days when movies were movies:
Captain America and Barbie in the flesh.
Wait a minute! I focus fast as they breeze by.
Nobody really looks like that—and who said they could!
On an all-white Harley, matching luggage on gleaming gold racks,
they burst the seams on our tidy patient rows of staid sedans.

Him—jut-jawed and keen-eyed, I'm sure,
behind those shades, but wearing what?—
white pants and, my god, a stars-n-stripes printed shirt,
wide sleeves billowing in the wind like sails.
And her—with only a brief excuse for a black dress hiked
halfway up her thighs, her bare back browning in the sun—
and a spread of bright gold curls tumbling
out from under her white crash helmet. Crazy, yeah,
but gutsy and gorgeous at eighty miles an hour.

As I turn to see the last of them, I want to raise an eyebrow:
There's no way he can keep those white pants clean all day,
and she'll have quite a burn on those sweet knees and shoulders
when they get to where they´re going, wherever that is.
Then I whip my head back to the traffic, and later,
turning off the interstate onto the county road to home,
I wonder what it would take to be invincible again,
what it would taste like to be brave and free.

The Taste of Honey

The chance to spread some sweetness
on the daily bread of someone else's life
draws us all, like flies, into saying yes.

But when the honey of promises congeals
into that sticky sludge, responsibility,
it seems impossible to get it off our hands.

It's like that old Red Skelton skit, where
the guy pulls the flypaper first off one hand,
then the other, then the other, until

we all lie gasping on the floor with mirth,
ending only when the show goes off the air.
Not fun at all is our own super-glued panic

that never-give-up can mean never-get-out.
And even never-let-me-go can harden
all too quickly into a never-ending story.

Artistic Vision on the Northern Plains

Outside Jamestown, North Dakota, a gigantic plaster cow,
high up on a bluff, overlooks the interstate traffic below.
In Harvey, a wealthy local wit built a huge grinning gorilla
to guard the town, or maybe keep an eye on the neighbors.
And the world's largest prairie chicken, a good twenty feet high,
stands sentinel at the entrance to Rothsay, Minnesota.

You can see, on any modest hill across the plains
of Minnesota, the Dakotas, and no doubt points west,
displayed with care, some farm implement of strange design—
ancient combines, old-world tractors, rusting harvesters—
abandoned? Possibly. But more likely placed there
to decorate the view, outlined against the stark blue sky.

Still the oddest sight, along the back roads, are those
boot-topped fences embellishing the edges of some fields—
aging split-rail borders, that suddenly, for fifty yards,
sport a bizarre array of old shoes, boots, galoshes of all sizes,
turned upside down on each and every fence-post. Why?
To make some use of things once valued? To conserve,

from some compulsive sense of thrift? Perhaps a cunning
prairie closet-artist's statement, using materials at hand,
to say that even the poorest scene is worth a look, a grin?
Or just a rural testament to kicking up your heels,
despite all-out survival mode? Or maybe a renewed resolve
to keep the land, with a kick in the pants to any who disagree.

Harvest Time

Driving at night through the flourishing fields
at the end of one more perfect autumn day,
I see the sugar beet harvesters still at work,
headlamps glowing on their huge tractors,
as they toil on through long hours of darkness.

They work steadily, urgently, determined
to use this brief balance of ideal weather—
sunny but crisp days, cool but gentle nights—
to gather the crop, so soon spoiled, at its peak.

The loaded trucks rumble down county roads
spreading a confetti of dust, dirt lumps, root debris
as they proceed, never minding the lights or path
or destination of small sedans like mine.

They are oblivious to my journey, at the end
of my own harvesting day, gathering promises
of funding from wary donors whom I've persuaded
to support the delicate growth of learning
on these remote but fertile northern plains.

But I too will spend whatever time it takes
to pull in all the goodness that is offered
when the moment is ripe. The beet harvesters
would not choose my toil, nor I theirs.

Yet I resonate with their labor, their rigor,
and I know their fierce devotion to the task,
because an accident of perfection demands
its own fulfillment, before the time is gone.

Blindsided

"Come this way,"
the sly snow whispers,
sliding sideways
across the icy highway.
The zigzag patterns
mesmerize you, lure your eyes
and your hands on the wheel
into unknown territories.

The whiteness teases,
wants you to follow
its slippery path
into the open fields.
An insistent wind
builds behind it,
nudging, edging you
toward the rising drifts.

You wrench your thoughts,
and the wheel, back
toward safety. Yet
the struggle continues,
and you begin to find
obscure comfort in
the give and take between
order and chaos. Until

the instant you look up
from the road
into the heart of
the whiteness,
and see too late
the dark stag, stock still,
looming just ahead.

Next Door Neighbors

We lived as next door neighbors for ten years,
her house about a long stone's throw from mine,
with both homes perched high up on rolling lawns
that led to gardens, benches, weathered decks,
and all our views focused on the clear blue lake.

Our parallel lives did not allow for chatter,
we both had jobs and families, all those homely
things that fill up days, and never more
than ten minutes to catch up in the midst
of family parties, potlucks, planting seeds.

While we could not spare the time for closeness,
I liked seeing her hive buzzing next to mine.
We sensed each other was the kind of person
you could depend on in a pinch—for things like
borrowed ice, lost dogs, and boat repairs.

It wasn't until I moved away, and years later
came back for an impromptu place to stay,
that we found ourselves in deeper kitchen talk.
She asked if I thought her husband was unfaithful—
that fearless leap, the distance breached, was stunning,

and her act of instant trust made me return the gift
with truth, with sharing other secrets from the past.
Now it makes me ache to think we might have
spent more hours nurturing each other's souls
in all those years of being such good neighbors.

Slow Fall

Each day for months I passed it going to work,
an old barn leaning plainly to one side,
its uprights slanting quite a bit off-center,
the doorway turning now from rectangle
to parallelogram, while its base
seemed planted firmly still in place.

It's not so odd to see a leaning barn
on country drives, even in good farmland.
The timbers weaken sometimes with aging,
things get worn, nails loosen, glue dries,
with windy days, rainy weather, summer sun,
or if the foundation is not laid just right.

But this one started to increase its pitch,
stretched its angle more and more. As
months went by, it turned quite marvelous
in its decline, its slow lying down,
its infinitesimal progress toward the fall,
defying gravity, it seemed, at the end.

Each day I'd think, *It's lovely in decay,
but it can't last much longer.* I'd vow
to bring a camera next time and capture
its amazing stretch, its improbable bend—
maybe show each phase, like that artist
painting a church in every season's light.

But then I got so busy I forgot it,
took a shorter route to town, and one day
a whole year later it was gone, flattened—
waste timber now, much like my intent
to record what I had seen, to reveal
the wonder of that long suspended fall.

Rickshaw Ride in Fargo

Coming out of a rehabbed, upscaled,
       overpriced downtown eatery,
shrimp and sherry still on our tongues,
       we pause to gaze at the spangled sky.

Laughing, loosened, lightened by
       uncommon girl-talk revelations,
we try to straighten up and get
       serious about finding our cars.

But a giggle bubbles up between us
       as we turn our eyes from the stars
to take in this—what?—this rickshaw
       parked on the walk in front.

The irony of it chokes up our mirth,
       we bump elbows in amazement,
and curiosity trumps disbelief
       as we peer into the cave inside:

Black leather seats, dark velvet mats,
       a gold fringe dangling from the roof.
A thin, young, college-scruffy guy
       steps out from behind: "Ride, ladies?"

We roll our eyes. "Five bucks an hour," he says,
       "anywhere you want to go."
He spreads his bony farmboy's hands
       in a mock footman's bow. We waver.

"We're too heavy, you couldn't carry
       two of us, we're going home."
"No problem, stronger than I look,
       just up the street and back,

and heck, why not?" Enchanted now,
        we clamber in with awkward hoists.
He steps between the two long poles,
        stoops to grip the handle bars.

We hold our breaths, lock eyes in glee.
        He lifts us, leans, takes a stride,
and we are transported—Forbidden City,
        Mysterious East, Orient Express.

He pulls with no effort, black wheels
        spin on either side of us
as he trots the pavement, up one side,
        down the other, just as promised.

Speechless with delight, feeling
        thighs stuck to leather seats,
breathing in the summer night
        with fringe rippling overhead,

we see a magic city for the first time,
        on this crazy, perfect ride
through the heart of downtown Fargo,
        if not Old West, perhaps New East.

Looking at Lines

This startling grid of light sharp lines,
shooting straight to the horizon,
is clear only from the air.
These right-angle roadways,
so even-spaced, divide and join
the regular, clean-cut farmlands
of the high Midwest—surveyed
flat out, no waste, no nonsense,
no time for curves or cleverness.

From above, the scene looks like
a powerful Mondrian mosaic
of light and dark: green squares,
beige oblongs, brown rectangles—
that secret code of what is fertile
or barren, fallow or flourishing—
punctuated only by a few
tight, thrifty clusters of white dwellings
tucked into the corners of the squares.

Then all at once, the astonishing
sight of curves, huge serpentine
bends—the lush, rich, dark green
windings of the Buffalo River—
becomes an intricate embroidery,
snaking back and forth and back again,
across the formal grid-like tapestry,
meandering in massive loops toward
its goal, the Red River—a complex ribbon
embellishing this modest box of land
with the promise of untold riches within.

Finding the Balance

Coming back to the heartland, I am again
struck by a sudden sense of balance,
a simplicity in this greening landscape,

where there are just the right proportions
of trees and fields, bushes and ponds,
to fit the hidden template in my mind.

This is my breathe-easy stretch of space
after leaving the east's complex networks
of tight-woven shores and woods and towns.

It can also be a comforting embrace,
upon returning from the west's wild sweep
of wide deserts, clashing cities, daring coasts.

Maybe this sense of home is just a trick
of early childhood memories kicking in—
hours of sprawling in such broad green fields

bordered by sheltering oaks, grass confettied
with speckled white-and-brown clover blossoms
begging to be woven into crowns.

Or it might be the sureness an artist feels,
sighing with relief, when the colors
ring true, when the large and small

and minute spaces clearly find the right
relationships, and when everything
in the composition finally fits.

II.

Nature's Flow

October Swim

Back floating, face to sun,
stirring icy waters with the pure
effort of my limbs, I leave
my body's warmth in the wake.

Swimming in bliss in this autumn gift,
looking up into the cobalt abyss
framed with lemon, gold, mustard,
cinnamon, blood-colored leaves,

my skin lowers its heat
to embrace the liquid's state
and, giving in to the chill,
becomes seamless with the water.

I slide through satin and see above me
the sky's silk split by one high-sailing tern,
dipping, turning, stroking the sheer blue air,
matching the current that moves me forward.

If the wind is right, I can float in the exact
pace and direction of the white wisps above.
Then the clouds and I move as one,
then all else is left behind, holding still.

Monarch in Exile

A monarch's hovering aimlessly,
rich orange and black, solitary,
along the margin of the water.

Odd, this late in autumn,
too cool for butterflies, don't they
disappear in weather under eighty?

Well, migration must take place
around this time, so where's his flock,
his flight, his swarm, his king's cortege?

Already off to Mexico? It seems
he's been left behind, too old
to journey, too frail to keep up.

His royal paisley papery wings
catch the waning rays of sun
and burst into jeweled light—

a magic instant. Now he lowers
himself to the damp sand, resting,
folds his glories for a moment,

then flies up again, landing
nearer to my hand each time.
If he lights on me, will I be

blessed? enchanted? or marked
to join this slow dance of death
he now parades before my eyes?

Sounds of Silence

I come to find the peace of quiet lake,
travel down this narrow maze of steps,
over a rocky, root-strewn, vine-filled pathway,
through the hovering net of shade-dimmed trees,
just to see and savor for a moment
the silvered surface of the waiting water
quivering silk-like in the light gray air.

The wind is nearly calm, the waves pause,
all forward motion seems transfixed in space.
Yet the woods behind me are alive.
They rustle, crack, snap with busyness—
whose? Just hectic squirrels shearing nuts
from brimming trees. Or crows knocking into
dangling branches poised to fall to earth.

Other creakings are the rub of limb
on limb, higher up where breeze gains strength,
testing joints of wood, stretching saplings,
without touching those below. A moment's hush,
and all knotted brows smooth out, listening.
Only then emerges the whisper of needles
on delicate twigs, the brush of wing on leaf.

A feather drifts to the ground and rests
on settling sand, where wind and water blend,
where ants still scurry silently—could I hear
their footsteps if I bent low enough?—
as they pile grain on grain to build a fortress
against the impending weight of distant snow
and the quieting of their humming lives.

Old Garden

It needed clearing badly—
I knew that from the beginning,
last year when I moved in. Yet,
aiming for trust, for optimism,
I decided to wait a season,
to see what might surprise me.

I started spring with the usual hope
and, bit by bit, discovered such
a homely jumble of promising
perennials and accidental annuals,
it seemed only fair to see things out,
let come what may by summer's end.

Now, late fall, it's too cold
for tough decisions, clearing weeds
and awkward plants like bee-balm or
astilbe that I never liked much
anyway. And everywhere are
fierce survivors I never noticed—

thistles, pigweed, upstart maple trees,
anchored with gnarled deep roots that set
their twisted tendrils many years ago.
I should have guessed as early as last winter
that this enterprise, dormant underground,
was a mixture of conflicting goals,

benign neglect, half-hearted inspirations.
I'll wait 'til spring, yet I expect a sadness
will come over me as I cut the lifelines
of these misshapen stubborn roots and then,
with some relief, send plow blades deep
to turn new soil and start to plant afresh.

The Night of Maples Falling

This is the night of maples falling,
enclosing travelers in a blizzard
of gold and red, joy and panic.
These leaves ripened through the fall,
waiting for the time to drop.
The birches fell two weeks ago,
the oaks will no doubt be much later.

But tonight, daggers of dark rain
and banshee squalls of gusting wind
tear maple leaves from summer's safe
apron strings, ready or not,
in mad kaleidoscopes of whirling
colored blades, with careless edges
flaunting five distinctive points.

As late cars cross the black-slick streets,
a fearsome wall of foliage rears up
in answer to some blind command.
By instinct, the drivers in a row
all brake, red tail lights popping on.
But there's no threat, just air's playthings
buoyed up this time by man-made wind.

The leaves seem amused to part for us—
we beings who interpret every
thing, who see all nature's motion
through our own flawed fearfulness,
and mistake the simplest truths,
with eyes wide shut, for evil perils,
as we hurtle through the night.

On the Way to Somewhere Else

Three doors of fresh-cleaned glass
look out on the wooden deck
overhanging this quiet lake,
a familiar trilogy of light.

But one day, as I made coffee
in the winter morning calm,
a sharp yet muffled thud broke
my parenthesis of peace.

Scanning the deck, I saw a small
dark form, no bigger than an egg,
crumpled up and oddly shaped,
lying on the sun-warmed wood.

I hurried out to see a gray-brown bird,
black beak, perhaps an early wren,
who'd flung himself against the glass
and dropped down like a stone.

I could not leave him yet for dead,
could not toss him out for trash,
could not with cringing fingers lift
him up to breathe the life back in.

So I squatted, waiting, seeing—
puzzled, looked around to find
some reason for his trajectory,
and spied one odd angle where,

coming in from deep left field,
he could've seen straight through the house
to a clear window showing sky
on the other side, a tunnel of blue,

sighting perhaps, as birds must do,
between the tangles of thick trees,
the next opening he needed
to make his way. I knew this:

He'd come in fast, seen open space,
dived into it head first (then heart,
then loins) until the glass, protecting
life inside that he could never know,

stopped him dead; his nut-like crown
took the impact, stunned him cold.
Yet I paused, in case there might be
a beat, a throb, within that speckled breast.

Soon I saw the small wings shudder,
rumpled head shake loose the darkness,
chest inflate with air, the whole thing—
miracle!—reconstitute itself. He then

took wing to nearest tree, not minding
the invisible that stops us all,
traveling those clear blue tunnels
on the way to somewhere else.

Winter Tryst

It's the last day of January,
winter's close to halfway through—
two months since I saw the lakeshore,
four since its water touched my skin.

The lake pulls me toward its sloping path,
my heavy boots ripple the softening snow;
careful here, not knowing what's beneath—
acorns, fragile twigs, slippery leaves?

In between the trees now, grabbing branches,
feet sliding, I sense the danger and wonder
if I should turn back from these tricky
little rocks and roots, treacherous moss.

Down at last to the edge, where pebbly sand,
still clean, greets me with a curving grin,
surprised yet wry, like last summer's lover,
and offers its damp verge for a welcome touch.

And the water—water!—it's half-frozen only
on the rim. Some sheer ice teases me, crackles
when I step on it, then turns to melting film
with ripples moving under it. But at the center,

it's all open, running strong and true and blue
with rushing current. I can't stay, so many
voices call me back. Still, on this halfway day
I know we'll be together again, all the way.

Small Shadings

Today the sun sinks down easy in its bed,
letting the sky's color loosen and seep
from buoyant blue to tarnished peach
to fading rose to brooding gray
in infinitesimal degrees.

It's like a beautiful woman aging, with just
a slight sag of the jaw, a fine net
etched with care on softening skin,
a once gentle mouth becoming
intangibly more resolute.

Each new stage can of course be guessed,
intuited from what has gone before,
as when a wrinkled bud unfurls its secrets
into a flamboyant burst of perfect petals
with just the edges starting to curl brown,

or when a flood of overwhelming need
subsides into a navigable river and,
much later, ebbs to traces in the sand.
Yet we seem to find in such small shadings,
again and again, the marvelous. We salvage,

from this endless progress toward the end
of things, some luminescent memory
of birth, some glimpse of the circle, in which
the human eye perceives—but never quite
comprehends—the dark blue of forever.

Almost Open Water

The last thin wafer of ice
that old winter laid down
across the trembling tongue
of the silent lake is melting,

like the ghost of a host
in the reluctant mouth
of a veiled communicant.

Under that stale gray shell
the water seethes, alive,
ready to swallow the crust
that chills its forces beneath

and stifles its vibrance within,
keen to throw off this ceiling,
this leftover, limiting lid.

I want to witness that instant
when the splintered crystals
submerge under new-born water
and the lake comes back to life.

Forward Scouts

After the bleakness of shifting snowfields starts to lift,
       after the fierceness of murdering ice storms has passed,
a day comes when the long-forgotten sound of geese whickering,
       far off, up high, begins to filter through the cloud layer
with those distinctive gabbling noise that sounds like
       No-orth? No-orth? No-orth?

You can't see but feel the flock of them flying overhead,
       necks stretched out, wind whistling past nostrils,
       leading with determined yellow beaks.
You can't see but picture the sturdy muscles in their shoulders
       beating the taut webs of their wings like metronomes,
       thrusting ever onward, with faltering not an option,
all following some bone-deep collective memory that calls
       Ho-ome? Ho-ome? Ho-ome?

If you focus in, you can almost imagine headwinds ruffling
       the fragile feathers of their cheeks,
airstreams tickling the longer silky wisps between
       soft underwings and downy flanks,
as they push on, each one following each of the others,
       voices fading now as you strain to hear
the last measure of their questing cries—
       He-ere? He-ere? He-ere?

Chasing Time

I am out of breath and patience.
Though tight-curled buds keep opening,
I can't slow down enough to catch up
with their minute, majestic unfurling.
I pant with hurry's exasperation,
flying too fast past ancient oaks
bearing their fragile lacy miracles.

I want to reach out and grab
Time by the throat, shake it,
saying, "Stop chasing me,
stop breathing down my neck."
I feel it nipping at my heels
until the whole world whirls by
so giddily my center loses hold.

I won't go faster, I will stop, suspended,
like a fetus pulsing silently
within the slowly perfecting womb,
like a last ripe apple bending at
the farthest reach of the smallest limb,
like a drop of summer saliva
on the quivering tip of a dog's tongue.

I will make myself slow down
enough to hear the single heartbeat
in my inner ear, as the right word
takes shape, emerges imperceptibly,
just like the first green blade
that inches through soft soil
and spears the air.

First Singer

Oldsters called it
rusty-gate bird,
for its simple
two-note song,
tee-wee . . . tee-wee.
It starts in spring,
with thin tones,
piercing sweet,
in minor key,
tee-wee . . . tee-wee.
It's the sound of
hinges squeaking,
doors opening,
may-be . . . may-be.
The chickadee
begins it all.

Ordinary Grace

You might see an old willow arching
        over the end of a terraced garden,
or a sunlit, cattailed lake shore,
        ruled by one red-winged blackbird,
or just a clearing sky that opens up
        far blue space beyond near green trees.

So simple—but you catch a quick sharp
        breath and think: Beautiful.
But why? Where did you get this power
        to be nourished by everyday splendor,
to recognize glimpses of beauty in
        such things as ordinary grace?

No use in taking easy refuge
        in some fantasy of Great Design
that sets you up to see only what's ordained,
        or some false philosophy of what
you see is what you get (and vice versa),
        or even what you want is what you see.

Reach instead into your memory depths
        and recall your own first infant chortle—
its well-spring lives on somewhere in your
        questioning, rational shell, ready
to let nature's familiar treasures
        release the delight that waits inside.

Listening to April

rubber   rebounding
hoop rims   clanging
kid calls   rising
gutters   trickling
snow crust   settling
cen ti me ter by cen ti me ter
into the spongy brown earth

sprouts   emerging
tires   whirring
wheelies   popping
geese   whickering
breeze   softening
mol e cule by mol e cule
into the downy gray dusk

Water Will Always Win

Water is relentless, impossible to stop,
easy to channel, simple to trap, but able
to carve its way over sand, around rocks,

through fibers, through cell walls,
adept at splitting granite, or hairs.
Water—delicate, flexible, light

in small doses, overwhelming
in tsunami-like waves—not hard but soft,
not always strong but continuing.

Determined, incessant, never-ending,
it wears its way down through the ages,
leaves a pathway clear for going on.

I crave its wetness on my tongue,
its playful buoyancy under my limbs,
its healing richness in my cells.

Let me begin to understand
what it takes to turn persistence
into power, to claim bending

as the greatest strength, to glimpse
the infinite inside the effortless
tiny dripping of joy on stone.

Angle of Light

There is an odd kind of crescent moon—
not the usual upright shining sickle
ready to slice through the onyx sky—

but one with a different tilt, glowing
at the bottom edge, looking
like a giant grin or perhaps,

as ancients thought, a glistening bowl
that could catch the night's rain,
and so they named it "wet moon".

It shows up only in winter
in the north, or midsummer
in the south, where once it caused

a wondering child, years ago,
to say, "Is that moon broken?
Daddy better fix it." Now grown,

she knows it all depends
on your unique slant, your angle
on the earth's curved surface,

your position in the hemisphere—
it's not so much a trick of the light
as a gift to the eye of the beholder.

Cloud Burst

These violent weather swirls, not predicted,
surprise us both, keeping us off balance.
All we want to do is go straight on, but
inside our eggshell car we're buffeted,
encircled by huge whorls of brewing storm.
With light sky all behind us, we push on
into the howling heart of watery darkness.

Great pellets of coarse rain smack down on us,
pull the solid ground out from under,
as downpour sheets the road with slickness.
Low-pressing demons of the smoldering air
smother our view, while wicked lightning forks
stab the swelling ground—again, again—
like vicious serial murderers of the earth.

Now lighter mists boil up like false hopes
ahead of us, out of the valley's depths.
We peer at steaming light on farthest edge
of a coal-dark sky—is the shroud lifting
inch by inch? Shreds of cloud creatures
trail their feet over the trembling tops
of the huddled, beaten, crouching trees.

We drive onward, bearing down again,
propelled at best by our hopeful knowledge
that somehow these endless rounds of beatings
will wear the beater out and have an end—
that somewhere, outside this seething cauldron,
beyond these fiercely blowing, spinning forces,
somewhere farther on there must be blue.

Poetry Ritual at the Frost Place

Artful voices analyze verse
inside the sacred barn's dark timbers,
full of needy dreamers, listening—

while I sit on the outer edge
with a split view, in awe of
burgeoning pastureland beyond.

Urgent words explain, past reason,
the inner shapes of poetry, yet outside
noon light behind soft breeze easily

defines broad leaf milkweed, fertile
seedy fronds, fine tangled grasses—
a wild multeity of summer textures.

Looking up, my drifting eye discerns
knotholes high in the old barn's walls
that let pieces of sunlight show through

like rough-hewn stars, while the wind
carries whispers in praise of greenness
into the shadows of our devoted day.

Out to the Reeds

The lake shimmers in the light north wind.
A patch of reeds a hundred yards or so from shore
forms a beckoning circle of tall green fringe,
and years of wondering rise up in me.

It's a perfect day to strike out alone
and reach those reeds at last—water's warm,
hardly a breeze, almost summer's end—
an easy swim on a careless afternoon.

The reeds grow from a sweet little sandbar
out there, I think, where even if the swim
seems long, I can rest, get my breath,
loll among the green stalks for a while.

I start out with strong, even strokes,
leave touch of toes on sandy gravel behind.
All in now, heart pounding with effort,
breath short. Sandbar in the distance,

reeds no closer, seem forever receding.
Slight twinge of fear: Can I do this? Sure
I can, no time to spare for silly panic,
calm and steady, don't turn back. Almost there,

I know the sandbar will give welcome rest.
Just two more strokes. I touch the first reed
and by instinct let my aching legs drop down,
down . . . down? There must be sand, but where?

My fingers feel the water close above me,
my feet touch on the soft muck far below,
more than ten feet down, still sinking . . . No!
Must get back up, find sky, find air—here!

I gulp clear light, shudder with betrayal.
The reeds hold no refuge for me, no respite.
They are their own world, tall and deep
and endless, not beckoning at all.

So tired, can I go back? No choice. I stroke on,
dogged, determined to save myself, knowing
clearly now no haven awaited me, a stranger
in a foreign element, and I head home.

The Long View

Okay, we get the big bang—
all the planets, stars, galaxies
expanding outwards,
bursting away, traveling
what seems like forever.

So we're on the ball,
but what happens next?
Is there some ending point,
some final scene dissolve,
or just eternal hurtling?

Then again, what if all
this is only one pulse,
one expansion, heading
for the eventual pause,
the running out of energy

at the outermost reach?
Why not then contraction,
pulled by combined gravity
generated by all these
throngs of cosmic bodies?

We might well be in for
another zillion years of
pulling inward. What if
right now we're just riding
one pulse that happens to go

outward, like one speck
in the universal bloodstream,
propelled by one lub, soon to
become a dub. Is that
the next big bang? Or
maybe that's eternity.

Light: Reflected

We are such creatures of the sun,
ever attached to its rays of life,
its heat the nest of our primal cells,
its light our mother, our early source.

It can give or withhold food,
direction, warmth, breath, and hope.
It can punish us with heat stroke,
blisters, blindness, savage drought.

Yet whatever reflects that light
grows more precious in our sight—
when we see a gleam that makes
an object shine inside or out—

whether glass or mirrors, clouds or lakes,
moonscape, fresh paint, golden coins,
polished jewels, or tight young skin,
or snow on boughs of ancient pines.

Perhaps each glimpse of glowing mother,
gives comfort to our doubting souls
that our complex clumps of cells
will continue, despite the dark.

The Penguin Paradox

Penguins can't help looking ridiculous—
waddling small-footed, belly-first, over the snow,
waving mini-flippers madly in a balancing act,
seeking forward momentum without flopping over
as they make their ungainly way down to the sea.

I know that feeling from far back in childhood,
awkwardly reaching for something precious,
knocking things over, bumping head first
into doorways, forging ahead, but knowing
(as if from the outside) the comical look of it all.

Yet penguins, just beyond the splash at the edge,
their clown-like belly flop into the depths,
transform themselves into the elegant aviators
life meant them to be, flying through water
with breathtaking arcs into beauty and power.

I skim only the surface of my lake, yet buoyed
by the elements, weightless as magic, I float
between water and air, transmuted by
infinite strokes of strange grace into flight,
like the dance of words on the page as I write.

The Circle: A Double Haiku

Look up: trees, clouds, sun,

endless sky beyond them all,

layers of heaven.

Underneath: warm wood,

cool waves lapping at the shore,

complete the circle.

III.

Family Gatherings

Molly in the Fields

I picture her with softly rolled-up shirt sleeves,
muscled forearms brushed with golden fuzz,
strong hands gripped tight around her weathered hoe,
and folds of her cotton skirt pooling on the earth
as she kneels among the plants she should be weeding.

Instead she's praying—head bowed, dark hair shining
in the hot June sun, eyes shut tight or staring at the sky—
Amalia, my grandma's oldest sister, they called Molly.
She was the favorite of their father, who began to hate her
because she defied his hopes, his fears, his needs.

"Let me just serve my Lord," cried Molly, standing tall
against his upraised hand. She burned to join the sisters
in the convent, the Carmelite retreat where she could revel
in the sacrifice of silence, and commune without words
only with her God, her one true love, for all her days.

"Why? Why should she not marry and bear children?"
came the roar from the throat of her crag-faced father.
"They cannot have her, not one so young and beautiful,
I'll give her all the farm, even now, today, forever!
She is my first, my best, she cannot waste this life."

Both hardened into rock by need, neither one could give.
Molly filled her stubborn days praying in the fields
for the love she could not have, until her spirit broke—
not her will, her mind. They brought her rigid, stone-like
to the asylum, where she spent her life locked in silence.

Stefan's Bedroom

He kept an evil-smelling pot beside his bed,
a black spittoon, shiny outside, slimy inside,
for the cough that racked him when he'd had
too many Marvel cigarettes pressed tight
between his brown-stained wrinkled fingers.

I liked to sit there, when I was three or four,
feet dangling, on the bed's thin-quilted edge,
while he told me stories of the Old Country
and how he got here on a boat in steerage,
with that great wave of 1890s immigrants.

At Ellis Island they took away his long Slavic name
and gave him another, with only five letters he could
learn to spell—not the same but close enough, they said.
I knew him just as Grampa, hard and bony, head bald
except a black monk's rim, his nose hooked and spotted.

His touch was kind when he called me *schatze*,
or *tootsi-li*, but his mouth became a tight line
and his eyes narrowed as he hissed and muttered
Croatian curses out the window, *jebemti-uuhh!*
and, when the church bells rang, *jebemti-kirche!*

"What do church bells say, Grampa?" "Hah, *mein schatze*,
they are ringing, *Bring dem geld! Bring dem geld!*"
("It means, 'Bring money'," Mama said, "don't you ever . . .")
And then we'd both sing, laughing, with the bells until
he'd cough, stomp a foot, and hawk at the spittoon.

Yet the oval photo by his bed held a different man—
sturdy, shoulders square in his serious wedding suit,
eyes dark and quiet, guarded, under black-brimmed hat,
and next to him, his plump-bodiced bride, solemn,
prepared to please, white-stockinged legs planted firm.

She bore him three strong sons, though she never left
her bed much after that first hard birth, my father's.
When she bled to death with the fourth one, stillborn,
Stefan forged his days in the iron foundry,
not in church, and the three boys raised themselves.

Now, years later, his life packed into our back bedroom,
he told his *schatze* tales, sang old songs, heard alphabets.
And the night my father, cleaning an empty rifle, blasted
a hole through the front door where I'd just played, Grampa
in his long johns held me tight 'til I stopped crying.

Song of the North

My Uncle Steve came back
when I was wide-eyed seven,
with his sunburned grin, strident voice,
full of tales from a two-year trek

across Alaska. A young man then,
out of work, seeking adventure
or luck, he hitchhiked up to Seward,
learned to use a dogsled team,

and vowed to see if he could make it
with his dogs across the ice
from Anchorage to Nome, before
anyone heard of the Iditarod.

Why? Who knows? Just to prove
he was tough enough to do it.
His stories were filled with Eskimos,
their skins like leather, their tight eyes

smiling, their igloos reeking with
wood smoke, sweat, and worse.
Some nights it got so bad he'd sleep
out with the dogs, hands and feet

buried deep in fur and skin-folds
to protect himself from frostbite,
and he'd watch the northern lights
rippling green across the midnight sky.

He ate their pemmican and muktuk
gladly, shared his own strong spirits,
and once he got the rhythm, began
to wish the trip would never end.

That came soon, when gangrene kissed
his frostbit toes, but he'd made his goal—
the Bering Straits, where you could look
across to Russia—so he returned

to cast his spells on us. The magic
drifted through his next sixty years
of hard work, scrapes, and alcohol.
So even though he ended up

demented in a nursing home
and no longer could remember
his old tales, his seeker's voice
still echoed in my ears, and I did.

Three Brothers, One Night

They had started out so close,
in age, in play, in hardships faced,
father an immigrant, mother dead.
No question that these three would brave
the world with scuffed shoes. Together,

they could dare to dive into a quarry pool
from a railroad trestle, or give a hidden
finger in a family portrait, or climb
a steel girder looking for a job.

Orphaned, married, fathers now themselves,
they had not spoken to each other in years.
What could have caused such total disconnect—
thoughtless words, imagined hurts, a chain
of actions and reactions escalating pain?

The oldest made a careless joke-for-real
to his youngest brother's wife, that their
daughter would more likely get knocked up
in high school than ever get to college.

The middle brother's devil was alcohol.
Consumed at every holiday, it loosed
his spiteful anger at his older sibling's
office job success, while he was still
coming home with dirty fingernails.

The youngest one most feared his fiery mate,
whose eternally offended heart made her
forbid a bedside visit to the oldest's wife
when she lay sightless inside a bandaged head.

And yet, one warm and tipsy Christmas night,
the middle son—possessed by a desire
to make things right—took it upon himself
to lure them all, by subterfuge, by luck,
into his kitchen, wives and children watching.

Though no words could ever take back earlier words,
he hoped that somehow reparation would be made.
Then, faces scowling, eyes touching, they felt
the old pull of blood, of skin, of shared breath.

They raised their arms to form a perfect circle,
clasping one another's shoulders. And when
they bowed their wordless heads toward the center,
their eyes gave them away by dropping tears
on the weathered wooden floor between them—

a sweet rain on that drunken holy night.
It would have to last them all their lives.

Perseverance

Grampa Charlie, smiling, squat, and square,
would come home bone-tired at night.
His nails rimmed with factory soot
on fingers made for playing mandolins,
he'd ease his aching muscles into well-worn chair.

Overshadowed, always, by his urgent,
take-charge, let's-get-it-all-done wife,
he fathered three wild boys, three earnest girls.
He stood on breadlines when he had to, ashamed,
but bore the Great Depression, persevered,

kept nose to grindstone, and provided
what each one hungered for the most.
Later, he made foreman, played the banjo
in a local band, delighted grandkids
with the tricks of rummy, solitaire.

He sent his first son, his finest one,
proudly off to battle, prayed for him,
kept all his scribbled letters from the front
in a wooden box lined with satin, then
welcomed him home, safe again at last.

The brothers celebrated that return
with an April fishing trip up north,
but they upset their boat into ice-cold lake,
and the hero, swimming for shore, cramped up
and drowned, just short, in three feet of water.

Grampa never blamed the war or God,
never lost his smile—except some mornings,
if you watched him lathering his face
to shave, you could see the silent tears
making channels down his foamy cheeks.

Missing Places

In my dream, the young man's face is shy,
with downward tilt of head, shadow of beard,
widening smile, yet behind it all, sad eyes—
and I know without a word he's homesick.

Not for family pain and poverty
that drove him out before his time. No,
he's missing a place he's never been before—
maybe a cabin high up in the mountains
with a wide open porch facing west,

where he and that girl from dancing class
somehow live together in quiet peace.
They'll cut each other's hair outside and let
the wind sweep the trimmings off the porch,
or sing a song before the sundown chill sets in.

My missing place? Probably more than one—
some I've lived and lost, some I've never had—
for sure the green-sloped shore and sun-baked pier;
that dappled pond with sandy bottom in the woods;
the seacoast house with broad veranda, grassy dunes.

And deeper than all those, my mother's quilts,
the contour of her warmth curved round my back—
I know it really happened, not just in a dream—
with her arm anchoring me gently as I slept.

Family Reunion

Busy in the city all these years,
it was easy to forget this place,
the old farm's family reunion spot—
gatherings every summer, lawn chairs spread
on bright June grass beneath the towering oaks,
kids careening 'round weathered picnic tables,
grown-ups arguing crops and politics,
baseball bats and gloves piled up for later,
sunlight warming oldsters' nodding heads.
I'm glad I brought my folks here one more time.

I stand in line, watching aproned aunts
dish up chicken legs and watermelon,
while a shirtless guy in overalls
swigging beer, wiping sweat off, tends
the old black sweet-corn roaster. Guess I'll get
three plates, filling up for Mom and Dad.
They came today after years away,
pried at last from their sunless condo—
but now they tremble, giddy and bemused,
among the swirl of shirttail relatives.

Good for them to get out more, I think,
to see familiar faces of the in-laws,
second or third cousins once removed,
shake weathered hands, pat downy cheeks, trade jibes.
They're getting welcomed back like prodigals,
forgetting the old hurts (if not forgiving),
filling in who died last spring, who married
in a hurry, who's back on the sauce—
eye squints, nods, and nudges all around—
and graying sisters squeeze in for a photo.

"I bet your mom and dad will win this year—
you know, the prize for oldest ones who came,"
says the cousin just behind me. *You're nuts,
I think, they're still going strong, in their prime,
I'm their kid and I should know.* Quickly
then my crowd-dazed brain calculates
the math. *Okay, they're in their eighties now.
Who else is older? No one? All passed on?*
When the serving lady kindly taps my plate—
"Jello, hon?"— I realize I'm next in line.

Ocean Views

Side by side we sit, looking
out at the far rim of the ocean,
close to the edge where each wave
slides up near our toes, and
peace rolls in to wash over us.

Together, we feel like sisters,
shoulders touching. I say, "I love
having nothing but water and sky
in my eyes—it makes my head
lean back, my breath go deeper."

She says, "It always disturbs me,
not being able to see across."
I say, "What?" She answers, "Lakes
are so restful, you know, where you
can see the trees across the water."

I ask, "What about that feeling
of freedom you get from seeing
no limits?" She answers, "That's
what I get from being able
to see to the other side."

Skating on First Ice

The lake has slammed shut overnight. The sun
bounces off the glazed and glaring surface.
We mourn the hibernation of summer's waves,
but we have a mission, my grownup girl and I—

we are determined to brave the lake again together
with ice blades tied on tight—to navigate the surface
if not the depths. With careful steps, aching ankles
wrapped inside stiff socks, no longer limber,

we wobble giddily, touch hands encased
in padded wool, not letting fingers intertwine.
We make our way down to the water, now
a slippery sheen. Yet here's the wondrous thing—

beyond our first steps off the crackling edge,
testing as we go, the icy floor's transparent.
If we look down, just below our trembling knees,
we can see everything, clear down to lake bottom.

The same six sheer inches of our frozen floor
becomes the translucent ceiling of the world below.
We see seaweed tendrils dancing in the undercurrent,
a fish shadow looming up between the rounded rocks.

Suspended over all, we begin to glide, uncertain,
seeking skater's rhythm, while across the lake come
those shocking, reassuring booms of ice expanding,
bonding strong. We move ahead and trust the flow.

My Barefoot Daughter Dancing

Today I see my barefoot daughter
dancing on the windswept beach,
swirling in her white bride's dress.
She hangs tight to her groom's
steady hands, leans back to see
the gulls wheeling overhead.
They both laugh as they circle,
capering on the grainy sand
delighting in their miracle.

Another time, some years before,
I watched her with a mother's gasp,
as she gave a calm testimony
to some newly found believers—
harsh words pouring out like grit
into my unbelieving soul—
about her journey up from hell,
how she'd longed to leave her life
until a savior's arms pulled her back
from surrender to the undertow.

Now I view this dance with gulls and sand
through ocean's haze, catching my breath
at how fragile are the strands
from each to each, then to now,
and how hard it is to understand
what makes them hold on, or let go.

Another Perspective

Now that age has blown their hopes
out of the water, and ill health
has scoured their dream of a better life,
they take the goodness left
at the heart of their bitterness
and shower it on me, beloved child,
growing elderly myself.

They yearn for me ardently now,
with the single-mindedness of a lover.
They hunger for the sight of my face
and their fingers savor the last
touch of my skin before I go.

They no longer assess me,
or criticize my choices,
as they once did when life
was young and the fierceness
of hope pumped in their veins.
Now grateful for the smallest kindness,
they treasure any gentle words from me.

So beloved, my love wells up
and threatens to swamp us all.
I swim now in this pure element,
which buoys, cleanses, overwhelms me.
Let me not begin to drown.

Practicing for Death

We practice saying yes to death
on withered plants that will not thrive
and seem to beg for plowing under,
or on small dear animals that have
stopped eating, started pacing
in pointless circles, lost control
of their soft bodies. We do know

that point—not clear at first but then
sure without a doubt—when death's
mercies would be welcome. So we kiss
their velvet heads, hold their paws
while the silent needle eases in,
look into their eyes that whisper
love and why and thank you. Yet

we still sit vigil with a father who
can now no longer eat, or breathe,
without the doctor's tubes and pumps,
in a sleep that will not wake again;
we make visits to the ghost of mother
whose mind has left her shell behind,
an empty locust casing on the lawn.

It would be merciful to hold their hands,
their faces, while the blessed needle
slips in to make them whole again.
If only we were not so cursed
with fears of our own last hours.
If only we could be as brave as dogs
and trust the one who lets us go.

Life's Work

I listen to the uneven hiss
of oxygen drawn in and out
by the old man's lungs,

rasping through the networks
of tubes—plastic and flesh—
that now make up his lifelines.

In and out, in and out,
it transmits a mixed message
that he is hanging on, with all

the spent muscles in his body,
to the life it's time for him
to leave. In the same way,

his strong and quivering hand
presses my fingers, sending
silent stories of love and loss.

His grasp tightens on mine, will not
let go. He breathes on, in and out,
and I breathe and wait with him

for the final effort and release
that will end his endless work.

Unanswered Questions

There are things I still want to ask you,
now that I'm getting older myself, things
I never could have said out loud even ten
years ago. Now you're gone but here goes anyway.

For one thing, did we drive you nuts about martinis?
We teased and chided, disapproved—and you
must admit they made you spill your anger freely—
but now I know their clean and slightly toxic beauty.

Also, how did it feel to drink your last one
when you swore off, after forty years on the road,
full of loud stories, wild nights, when you knew
your worn-out gall bladder could take no more?

This one's hard: Did you make love to that French girl
whose picture you saved among your army souvenirs?
And why did Mother let you keep it? Or was that
the nurse who brought you through the shrapnel blast?

Can you tell me what the nightmares were, the ones
that made you sit straight up, stunned, in your bed,
wordless and sweating, looking through the wall,
when you came back home, long after Normandy?

But why did you never want another child,
even though you seemed to see me as a treasure,
although mother begged you hard in storms of tears
and plotted ways she could conceive by trickery?

What did you lose by giving up your studies,
your pursuit of evolution in your college years,
to go to work in railroading, in order to support
an angry father and two freeloading brothers?

And when did you know you'd never get to Africa?
Did the dream of gazelles crossing the sunlit veldt
still plague you during those nights after the last stroke,
nights of numbness, wet sheets, labored breathing?

All these questions are too late. Just now, when
I've wised up enough to let you teach me, you've gone
and left me here, trying to fill in the blanks. I think
I know the answers, but I want to hear you say them.

After Images

If her withered mind blurs
the outlook of today, at least
let her remember lakes
gleaming in afternoon sun.

Let her remember small green
apples that fit in the hand,
too tart to eat but promising
sweet flesh to come in the fall.

Let her recall dandelions
wilting in a child's tight fist,
and grass stains on her dress
from kneeling down to play.

Let these images, almost lost
but lingering on the mind's film,
be pictures she sees one last time
before the darkness covers all.

Too Much Light

This day's beauty
hurts too much
with fresh pain.
The person she was
is here no more.

Pearl-colored
November sky
opens for sun
to warm the world
but only drives
the hurting deeper.

I see in the depths of
my mother's blank eyes
what I will become.
Hide me, shield me
just for this day,
to shade the sight,
to dim the vision
I know will appear.

Momentum

The year's first day is cold, clouds are clearing,
new snow hides the last storm's bumps and ruts.
Visiting grandkids clamor to go outside and play.
Mind on cooking, I wrestle with boots and scarves—

Where are their moms? Who'll keep an eye on them?
Will they be safe alone? Oh, well—it's just
our yard. Too old to join in snowy games,
I turn to tend the sizzling feast, and yet

the window's nostalgic view pulls me back.
Only six and three, they've hauled out the sled,
the old red-and-yellow one stored in the shed.
They are siblings, rivals, fierce competitors,

but here they are, taking turns pushing off,
sliding down the gentle hill, trudging up
together, sled between them. Then—and how'd
they think of this?—they both climb on, in tandem.

It goes faster now, more weight, gains speed,
but too much! Their angle's changing, heading
straight for the corner's huge old oak—Oh, no!
Paralyzed at the window, I can't get to them.

Then, last minute, they both ditch by instinct,
each jumping sideways just in time, shrieking,
buried in white, emerging, brushing each other off,
climbing back up the hill. So I'm out there now,

barefoot in the snow: "I was so scared, you should come in."
Their dark eyes sparkle up at me: "We want to go again."

On Grief and Gratitude

These infant herbs have all died of thirst,
neglected while I played with growing grandkids.

I'd watered them for days with so much hope,
but now their green shoots of life form dry webs
and crumble under my touch, as I stop caring.

My mother died two weeks ago, her systems
shutting down from Alzheimer's and old age.

The nursing home, hospice people, and I
(flying back and forth for twelve long years)
took such good care of her, now only ashes.

The grandkids fill these days with silly laughter,
urgent needs for look, look, Gramma, right now!

My spirit, thirsting for my mother's touch,
wants to wither, just decay, blow away, but
instead takes root in this rich soil and springs forth.

Cicada Song

In the shelter of the humming trees
that surround our crumbling cottage,
we savor soothing sounds of a hot day
coming from the whirring of cicadas
sawing away at summer. "Hear that?"
I ask the child leaning against me.

"What? Where?" "That little ringing,
fizzing, singing sound behind the leaves."
She cocks her small head, silky hair
dangles over one eye, and her mouth's
corners turn up: "I thought it must be
just the air—what makes it do that?"

"Little creatures like beetles" (the mouth
turns down) "called cicadas," I say. "They live
a long time underground, then come up
to live a short time in these old trees,"
I go on, "before they split their shells
and come out new, with wings. Then

they find mates, have babies, and die."
She says, "They sound like the choir
in church—are they singing to God?"
"No, it's just the males calling to the
females to come and find them soon."
The small brow furrows: "But why?"

"Look," I say, "here's one already gone."
Her eyes widen at the clear amber husk
resting in my palm, still a perfect replica
of its owner, with one small slit to show
where it slipped through and took flight,
never minding what was left behind.

IV.

On the Move

The Surprises of Waves

Ocean surges, water dances,
light plays on the pockets of smooth sand
between the age-old boulders scattered on the beach.

Incoming waves rush up fast,
slide at random angles over rocks beneath,
by turns to relax, alarm, or assault those who watch.

That brief time of surging forth
could be the length of a human lifetime as it
reaches out, transforms, slips back, reorganizes.

Only the rocks stand firm
as the eons sculpt their minute changes,
while sand flexes and regroups with every massive roller.

One Speedo-clad old man
with strong legs, browned skin, furry back,
climbs (by god) barefoot over the gray impassive stones.

May he not let his sinewy foot
be caught between the hulking hoary boulders
and bruise or break those tender aging matchstick ankles.

Yet he springs deft from stone to stone,
then reaches a smooth space and pauses, breathing,
before he leaps, grinning, to the next knot of ancient rocks.

Pulling Anchor

Those storm clouds boiling up like steam behind us
were not here this morning, even an hour ago,
when we began this ocean fishing venture
in a second-hand boat with rehabbed hull,
so certain of our skill and destination.

Now a vicious chop surrounds our little craft,
and we bless the strong brass anchor holding us
as we abandon poles to start the engine,
to make a run for land against the wind.
What, no homeward hum? No spark at all?

The old motor coughs and dies. My partner
tinkers, dropping tools. I pay out anchor line
because the swells are rising, eight-foot now,
and the small boat's bow needs play to ride
the raging peaks and troughs that buffet us.

My mind's eye sees the anchor, gleaming darkly,
dug fast into the sand below, rock-firm,
but the swells are ten feet high and climbing,
and we pray each peak will break before the bow,

not swamp us as the boat lurches steeply
down between the monstrous water walls.
I've let out all the anchor line there is,
and still the sea towers, winds scream on.

"Pull up the line," he yells! "I can't," I shout back,
"it's wedged, and if I do, we'll blow to Cuba!"
"Just cut it, or the next wave will be our last!"
I saw forever on the thick rope, picturing
the brass weight tight against the reef below,

our safety and our doom. The last hemp thread
frays and snaps, the small boat rights itself,
and we give our fates over to the mercies
of the winds, the swells, as we break free
and turn our sights toward the clear horizon.

Judgment Call

This guy I'm driving with, he just
makes me crazy with his driving.
I know, I know, it can be
a judgment call for when to switch
lanes in this interstate race
to get on with it and get there.

But he'll wait, fuming, in a right-lane
pocket, for some quick and careless
guy to pass him on the left.
Then he'll gun it as he slides
out to the left, nearly scraping
the other guy's back bumper.

After miles of such jockeying,
when finally there is open road
ahead of him in the left-hand lane,
he'll pull back in on the right. Then
the whole charade begins again!
At last it hits me in the gut:

He can't deal with really open road.
Some self-destructive devil inside
makes him pull back, just when
he could surge forward, have it all.
Instead he re-deposits himself
in a familiar painful pocket,

while others get ahead and make
him wait. The truth, the real kick is
this guy, my husband, drives me wild
but also gives me easy ways
to find my own pocket, where I've
just pulled in and put myself, again.

Antique Shop Questions

Old things, edges wiped and buffed,
priced to sell, lure us as we shop
on this suddenly rainy weekend.

Pockmarks polished, scratches shined,
dust removed from wooden grooves—
behind it all, I see grains of history
still embedded in their pores.

But what history? and whose?
Are these nicks from a loving family
playing with dominoes 'til dawn,

or rhythmic jabs of a dry pen point
made by a bored boy marking time,
or dagger scars of a woman waiting
to confront her faithless lover?

How can I admire or absorb
this silent residue of other lives—
under a guise of thrift or style—

while the rebel still alive in me
aches to snub the old, the revered,
yearns for the clean, the new, the pure,
to burnish with my own life's destiny?

Just Before Landing

We traverse huge piles of cumulus clouds,
white frothy whipping cream mountains of clouds,
as if aerosol-squirted, mounded up high
on giant dessert trays of free-floating thermals.

And here, there, are small puffs of strays
scattered about like over-spilled dollops,
across the far-off broad green tables
of familiar flat land somewhere below.

By tiny degrees we drop down between pillars,
admiring these close-ups of puffy skyscrapers—
sun-sculpted structures with edges aglow.
As we sink lower, slowly descending,

at last below them, we look up—really
at nothing but plain gray cloud bottoms
that create the dull sky-cover over the city.
We who saw miracles moments ago

now lower our sights to fast-rising pavement,
hiding our usual small trickles of fear,
bracing ourselves for the bump underneath
that will signify solid, welcoming ground.

Ascent in Albuquerque

With a burner's flare heating
the air inside each balloon's belly,
we all wait in the Albuquerque predawn.
Jets of flame leap upward into the near-darkness,
a roar rolls across the high plains desert, again, again,
and fire seems to erupt everywhere over this gigantic field.
Each brief but intense glow illuminates a sea of eager watchers,
all eyes wide, mouths open, leaning forward into dawn's chill air.
The balloons' rainbow colors and strange shapes begin to swell
in magic contours of red and orange, green, purple, some like
clowns or ducks or possibly Darth Vader, while confident,
impatient pilots begin to climb into their waiting baskets,
and their loyal crews beneath them break into cheers.
As the darkness goes on lifting, turning the air
to misty gray, filling our hearts to bursting,
we stand in awe of balloons pushing up
against their tethers, hovering
just above the ground.
Then one by one they
lift off, leaving fires
and crew and crowd
behind as they soar
upward into silence.

Launch footnote:
over 700 balloons
filling 54 football fields,
seen by crowds of 50,000,
took off in less than 2 hours.

Aspen Song

I see the wind
sweeping across these high peaks,
stirring mountainsides to life,
rustling through autumn-gold aspens,
lifting their gilded, sun-drenched leaves,
spreading sequins of light over dark green pines.

I hear the wind
whispering messages from the sky,
sighing through the trembling leaves,
tickling them from underneath,
until they dance, sing aloud,
turn new sides to the streaming sun.

I feel the wind
stroking old memories under my skin,
as I tremble on the stem of the past,
waking old hopes, soothing old pains,
until I rise, gleaming, lit from within,
and turn a new face up to the sky.

I am the wind
coming from nowhere, gaining force as I go,
rousing the depths of old-growth dark forests,
scattering flashes of blazing gold sparks,
caressing the slopes of the mountainsides,
leaving no trace but the sigh of the leaves.

Above Angel Fire

Dawn drifts in on silent wings,
a pale gliding specter of silver light.
It fills this valley between deep woods
with rising billows of pure white mist
that cushions the waking of all beneath.

The mist takes on a mysterious presence—
maybe clouds from above, or steam from below.
It floats and shifts in fantastical shapes,
like layers of heaven slipped briefly down
to soothe the earth, to fill its dark voids.

Then fingers of fog among silent trees
seem to reach upwards, longing for home.
These almost invisible smoldering wisps
form ghostly feathers of ascending smoke,
flickering up in the heat of the sun.

Are they merely warm soil breathing into cool air?
Or conjured by spirits to give us all hope?
Or warnings that what is pure does not last?
Perhaps their task is to comfort the feet
of hovering angels who cannot touch earth.

On the Road in Mexico

The air pulses with mesmerizing rhythms,
hard and soft, of the land in central Mexico.
Aztec-laden sounds and tastes permeate
the place names: Xochimilco, Tlalnepantla.

High rocks, grassy ledges, old mountains
are scoured away by hot winds, with only
their cores standing now, like monuments.
More road signs: Oaxtepec, Tlayacapan.

Hills are wind-carved into fantasy shapes—
tables, castles, spears, elephants—
and in between, every fertile inch
near Puebla, Cholula, Chalco, Zacatepec,

is cultivated with *nopales*: flat paddles
of green cactus (delicious simmered
with *chipotles*) reaching for pale blue skies
above Chapulco, Totolalpan, Iztapalapa.

Hills unfold to reveal more villages—
Cuautla, Cocoyoc, Chichinautzin—
small scruffy towns full of three-legged dogs,
balding horses, heedless children, weathered men

staring from the crooked, darkened doorways.
Back out on the highway, shaggy corn fields
mix with graceful sprays of sugar cane
near Acuexomatl, Zeopapalotzin.

Far off, rain trails on two volcano tops, where
Popocatapetl, "the mountain that smokes,"
stands sentinel, waiting for his lifeless lover
Iztaccihuatl, "the sleeping woman," to awake.

A Betrayal of Flowers

The callas that my love gave me long ago
were not faded like these lilies from the streets.
Unable to rise above this betrayal of flowers,
I toss the blossoms out the car's open window
into the crowded slums as we drive by.
There they are eaten by hulking shadows,
engulfed by a flood of weeping leaves,
set aflame by the fires of raging eyes.
The memory of his promises to me
blossoms across the fields in my head
into a million prayers—not to heaven
but to treacherous time—so precious,
taken for granted, ripped from our lives,
thrown to the four winds. Time persists
in withering all the lilies, so like his face
that crumpled into itself as he turned away
from me and joined the gardens of the dead.

Healing Armando

He had come to be cleansed, seeking a place
to bathe the wounds of greed and lust and anger
that festered in his soul after ten years running drugs,
ricocheting from street to prison and back again.

He entered this house in anguish, to ask a gentle man
with searching gaze, strong and quiet wife, wide-eyed
little girl, newborn babe, and naive *gringa* guest
to help him decontaminate his life and start again.

I wondered how he could erase the years of violence
and dare to spew his past on untarnished lives?
The words of when and where and how and why
flew between penitent and pastor, hesitant

at first, then gushing out in a harsh stream
that could threaten to engulf the innocent
as well as the guilty, the gunfire pace of Spanish
spraying sins against the wall, until a clear space

appeared in his eyes. Exhaustion. Then a meal.
A place for him at the table. His handshake to me
felt hard, like gripping a rocky ledge and looking
farther up to climb the sheer cliff behind his eyes.

I said, "Where you from, Armando?" in my faulty
Spanish, and I saw the hardness in his eyes
soften one or two degrees, while we struggled
to parse each other's words and find some meaning.

When did the cleansing happen? While I knew little
of churches, washing sins, or even forgiveness,
I could feel his scarred soul loosening, stretching,
sense his battered heart easing open in the warmth.

Later we saw he left behind a package, wrapped
with care. We thought it might be for the baby,
but it was a hand-made cardboard sign saying,
"Bless those who can forgive without asking why."

Crossing the Masai Mara

Long, lazy grasses whisper secrets
under this truck's unyielding frame.
Midday sun bakes a herd of small gazelles
sprinkled like flowers in the rippling field.
The air wake of our truck makes tiny birds
fly up and blow away, like iridescent
confetti, over the searing hot savannah.

Umbrella-spread, the single-trunk acacia trees
are spaced across this stretch of arid plain—
like curios displayed upon a shelf,
or ballet dancers pausing on a stage,
or thumbtacks marking targets on a map—
why this wide span? Is it because scarce rain,
sparse soil, can support only survivors?

Urgent questions flit across my brain pan,
diving and vanishing like the elusive birds.
I try to capture darting words on paper,
but dusty wind evaporates the pen strokes,
wild bouncing truck condenses the phrases.
Like carefully spaced acacias,
only the strongest can survive.

Stalking

At dusk in the valleys of Kenya, we're stalking the leopard,
peering through endless layers of leaves just to glimpse
his dappled velvet, his deep golden eye, his sleek ripples
masking sinewy coils of surprise and death. Perhaps
he is gliding right now, belly low, in the silken grass
that billows behind this delicate herd of impala.

We imagine him springing with swift execution,
the razor-sharp claws piercing sweet chestnut hides,
twisting the necks graced with lyre-shaped horns.
We picture the curved yellow teeth sinking into red flesh
still pulsing with life. We secretly throb with the image,
the speed, the loss, the shock of the possible kill.

Instead we spy, high in the crook of a wide-spreading tree,
the chewed dangling haunch of last night's superfluous kill,
his leftovers, tucked away from the scavenging mobs.
So we wait, as he waits, perhaps in sated sleep, behind leaves
somewhere below, drowsing in brush. At last hunger
drives him to rise from his blind, to gather, to pounce

up the tree trunk to where he now stands, full height,
balancing on a single bare branch, outlined in twilight,
sickle moon and one evening star up above. Our ears flinch,
hearing him rend the dark flesh, gnaw the white bone.
Our eyes, appalled and enthralled, feast on the scene,
while one patient hyena circles below.

The Intruder

I am an intruder, I know,
unwitting, unwilling interloper,
stepping into the cheetah's netted pen
while a guide from the sanctuary
beckons me to join him without fear.

My heart drums inside clenched ribs.
I crouch behind this hand-raised cheetah,
abandoned child of the wild, seeming tame,
encircled by webbed steel on earthen floor,
canopied with dusty green branches.

The guide prods me forward, nearer cheetah,
with gentle reassurance. I reach out
pale fingers to touch his spotted crown,
just as he reaches his head back toward me,
housecat-like, to get his ears scratched.

The drumming flow between us smoothes
to humming. I bury my fingers in his fur
and tickle the spot I know that all cats love.
I feel his warmth, as he feels mine.
And then the purring begins.

Africa in My Eyes

Flaxen grass, chocolate rivers, deep jade thickets,
far hills in shades of mauve, smoke, azure, indigo,
molten dawns, glinting moons, black velvet nights—
the colors of Africa come back to me in sleep.

The eye records a range of tones and shades that the finest
camera captures only in colored dots, as reassembled pixels;
the living lens can coalesce life's sweep, its moving image,
while the camera locks perfection in one brilliant instant.

Behind my eyelids now, each time I close out daily life,
I see the sun-drenched dusty hues of Kenya's grasslands—
tawny flames of lion's mane fanned to blond by scorching winds;
cheetah's fur a mirror of the Rift Valley's tree-spotted plain;

sand-dune ripples of impala shoulders tensing for the chase;
black-and-white exclamation streaks on the honeyed haunches
of poised Thompson's gazelles forming cryptic hieroglyphs;
blue-jean-hipped plump topi herds ambling through the fields;

mud-brown hides of wildebeests draped in royal folds;
and charcoal hulks of cape buffalo pawing dung-dyed earth—
all this, against the sun-bleached, near-white crests of moving grass,
surging like ocean foam up the steep sides of the stony cliffs.

Yet the tides of dawn and dusk drive all, and finally
there comes a softening sadness on the light's last edge,
so that blade by blade, hair by hair, all colors become one.
Then invisible hunters take, in death, what life needs to go on.

V.

Between Two Worlds

Lie Down in Moonlight

I lie down in moonlight,
my back to the earthly lover
beside me in the rumpled sheets,
my face to the mythical one,
starry Orion just arising

in the late September night.
He reclines on the horizon
large and looming, on his side,
in mirror image, in my mind,
of my own reclining body,

arms and legs flexed, alert,
the three cold stars on his belt
aligned in perfect angle with
the three warm scars on my breast.
While my breathing lover sleeps,

I turn toward the shining one,
separated only by silk gown,
sheet, curtain, window glass,
tree branches, and a hundred
thousand miles of midnight space.

The moonglow spins a silvered web,
electrifying all who are awake
and seeking in this pre-dawn hour,
fusing human and cosmic signs
into a single universal ache.

Touching at the Edges

In the early days of bliss, he gave me
two bright coins and said, "Imagine these
are us, where would you put them on this table
to show the underlying nature of our love?

Individual coins with space between?
Stacked up, one above and one below?
Overlapped with separate but shared space?
Side by side, touching at the edges?"

Well, I knew imagery as well as he,
so I hesitated, seeing rights and wrongs
strewn in my path like mines beneath a field,
weighing independence against romance.

Then, being young, I went all out for love
and stacked the coins as one, fitting tight,
as I said, "Our partnership will blend us,
lift us higher, make us one new whole."

A quirky eyebrow raised, he said, "Here's mine."
He took apart my coins and spread them,
separate but together in one place,
side by side but touching at the edges.

So my thoughts of oneness fell apart,
my dream of two lives merged, of sleeping
curled into a single spoon, dissolved,
but I held my peace and smiled a bargain.

While we never slept as one (he needed space),
I came to relish this expansion of body and mind—
the separate accounts, the times alone, the grace
to lend our hearts but keep them to ourselves.

In our graying, the double and the queen-sized
beds have both gone by the way, replaced
not with a king (his legs twitch in the night,
I fling my arms around, we both might snore)

but with two singles: twins, side by side,
edges touching, separate springs and linens,
one wide spread covering all. There we find
the peace that can be known only in dreams.

Healing

His artist's fingers traced the swelling curve
of my round young arm when we first met,
pausing at the small bloom of a bruise,
touching tiny scars never catalogued.
"Where do these come from," he asked in wonder.
"I bruise easily," I said, "I heal slowly."
He laughed: "I guess I better handle with care."

He, on the other hand, I've come to learn,
stops bleeding in the instant trauma ends,
whether by surgeon's knife or colleague's
spear or supervisor's silent cuts.
He has a child's capacity to forget
the mutual injuries of our time together,
the kind inflicted by betrayal of the heart.

Those hidden wounds, yes his, yes mine,
blossom outwards in ripples of pain,
and in their subsiding, their healing,
engender anguish and relief at once—
starting with the chilling heat of anger,
then the itch that masks the end of hurt,
finally the dim glow of forgiveness.

Now, in the cadence of our years together,
both dark and light, music and silence,
we find the rhythm of our lives again.
Beyond the eye for eye, mine or yours,
our souls rekindle and flame up, both
in retribution and in celebration,
burning steady for the night ahead.

Traitor

The body's betrayal begins slowly,
perhaps with a single tick
at the back of the brain,
a first red blink that signals
the breaking of the code:
a spark missing its leap between neurons,
one cell wall crumbling silently,
a dub instead of a lub.

Such warnings, first ignored,
then all too clear in retrospect,
whisper that treachery's afoot.
Quietly, hidden—easy to overlook
as shadows moving through the trees—
comes the turncoat, snipping the barbed wire,
dismantling defenses in the dark,
to clear a path for the enemy.

In time, he makes his move,
takes his advantage in the open:
a wave of weariness lasting a moment too long.
a flood of passion ending a moment too soon.
So topples this flimsy fence we build
against the circling winds of winter,
making way for the measured march
of cold leather boots
into the heart of the city.

Do You See What I See?

This sleek little six-seater plane
gathers speed, leaps into air,
leaving summer treetops behind
on its way to escape from real life.

The rippling depths below us,
aqua, turquoise, indigo,
steal my breath, spin my head,

and I turn to see if you see
how beautiful the moment is—
but there's just an empty seat.
Anyway, you would have said,

"Oh, beautiful? That's too easy,
you romanticize everything,
tell me what you really see."

So beauty's not enough for you—
you want reality? How about
the choking sounds at three a.m.
I heard beside me in our bed?

How about my frenzied call to 911
with phone clamped to my shoulder
as they instructed me in CPR, while

my fingers pinched your stubborn nose,
my lips forced breath into your mouth,
my fists pounded hard and urgent
on your chest—too high? too low? No—

My eyes would rather memorize
the azure layers of this lake,
the sandy shores of this island.

Yours, I guess, will keep the white
light of God or the crematorium
as their last sight. And yes, I know,
we always did see things differently.

Of Love and War

In the early days they fought like ancient enemies,
        he bent on power, she with hidden knowledge
of his weak spots, each feeling that their conflicts
        would be part of future daily life.

They both thought military war—the kind that nations
        declare upon each other—was surely evil,
a backward, even primitive urge that should be
        channeled into something more productive.

So when the government letter came (back in days
        when there was still a draft) telling him
to report for army induction, they hunkered down:
        No way, no how, yet clearly no escape.

The night before his physical, when she felt him
        shivering in bed with terror, sudden tears
running down his face, she took him in her arms,
        until her love calmed his pounding heart.

When he returned next day with goofy smile
        and stamped release (he was 4-F, unfit to fight),
she took the would-be warrior in her arms again,
        felt her defenses melt with new accord.

She could not know that forty-some years later
        his brave imperfect heart would stop short
under her pleading helpless hands, and leave her
        with the memory of their treaty, but no peace.

Empty Spaces

Empty chair at the holiday table,
vacant side of the marriage bed,
urn of ashes stored in the closet,
for some as-yet-unplanned farewell.

Clouds ask the chill night sky:
How can nothingness be real?
It's no more possible than
looking up to see a star missing

from a well-known constellation,
like the bottom corner of the dipper
erased—a sudden hole where all
that cosmic water can leak out,

leaving us with eternal thirst.
Dark sky replies: Or how the joining
of sickle moon and brilliant Jupiter
briefly graces a bleak winter evening,

but gone by spring, is not expected to
return for another thousand years.

Up and Out: A Dream

The first few yards
    of climbing upward
out of this dark pit of grief
    are impossible.
The walls seem perpendicular,
    there's no incline,
    no slant on which
    to get a purchase.

Yet images of gleaming teeth, hot breaths,
    just below my tears, seem to supercharge
      my scrabbling fingers,
      bunched shoulders.
      damaged knees,
      aching thighs.

At first there's only dirt of the past, packed tight,
    wedging up into my fingernails,
    ripping cells from my elbows,
    filling up my squinted eyes.

Then a bit farther on, here,
    I touch the first tiny shreds
of spreading root systems,
    tracking outward from the base,
    and I grab on,
ripping most of them to pieces
    on my way up. No matter,
    if they can save me.

At last, as soil rains down
        upon my contorted face,
            I latch onto thicker tendrils.
I twist their wiry vines
        around my aching fingers,
while they loosen harsh stones
        that scrape my knuckles,
stretch the tendons
        in my ravaged wrists.

But I care not at all,
        because just above,
        just here, are
        even stronger strands
        that lead to nourishment
        and sun-washed air.

I will not stop until I reach
            the taproot,
            which I know
            I can follow
            all the way
            back up.

Only then will I
        be able to get a leg
            over the grassy rim,
                stretch out full length,
                    and breathe again.

No Answer, No Message

One of the hidden benefits you get,
losing your oldest pal, your lifelong mate,
is that now, at long last, at very least,
you have no one else to answer to—

no mother peering into your school bag,
no father waiting up with furrowed scowl,
no spouse with probing pauses, sullen moods,
no kids with needs or wants or crazy fits—

really no one to question what you said or meant,
where you were, or what you did or didn't do,
what you were thinking, or not thinking,
how long you'll be, why you were short.

There's no call, no push, no pressing need
to answer all those pointless questions—
just the tangled darkness of your own thoughts,
the blinding light of truth inside your dreams.

In time you see there's no time left, no chance,
to answer what was once called for so urgently—
why you looked, why you didn't look,
why you cared, why you didn't care.

In truth, you don't care anymore because
there's all the time left in the world,
no one to answer to,
no one to call,
no question,
no answer,
no more.

Three Clearings

Hunting through mazes of memory,
I find tangled, verdant pathways,
connecting with no open gates,
dead-ending only in tiny clearings.

In the first, the scent of pine
lingers from a wet encounter,
where my tender back welcomes
prickles from tree debris fallen
on the forest floor under pressure
of our ardent bodies, while above
a strange new bird song rings.

In another, I lie alone this time,
on a quiet lakeside beach
with each grain of sand gritting
into my aching rigid calves
and tight shoulder blades, as water
seeps from the corners of my eyes,
at the image of his blind betrayal.

Then, a leafy scene appears,
a verge of wild trees bordering
an ancient, somber spread
of granite-marked remains,
where a small opening in the earth
will hide the ashes of his silent spirit
from the distant brooding mountains.

I feel again those thick green blades
under my knees, as I lean forward
to touch the marble urn one last time
before the merciful dirt covers all.

One More Day

A good friend's mate has heard his verdict:
      brain tumor, no hope, no way.
As they try to savor the time that's left,
      make the most of every moment,
a phantom in her own brain whispers:
      What's ahead, how bad, how long?

Is her grief different from my own
      when my mate departed in a flash,
choking in the night, as his heart's
      transmission dropped, then stopped?
I reached over unaware, and poked him,
      hissing: Stop that snoring.

Now she lives the time-warped life
      of seize each moment, foresee the worst,
the love-warped life of weep for every touch,
      embrace every jolt of pain,
both real and foretold. The loss is coming:
      Surely not yet? but when? but why?

Is it better to know, to prepare a place
      for death, learn letting go in small degrees?
Or not to know, go numb with disbelief,
      untangle an aftermath of papers, banks,
lawyers, under a cloud of nameless fears,
      looming hardship, causeless chaos?

Both groups of friends have uttered all
        the careful proper platitudes:
At least you can get ready, find the will,
        have a chance to say goodbye. Or:
At least he didn't suffer, you were spared,
        it's by far the best way to go.

She must wish that she could have it over,
        no more doubts, no wondering what to do.
I still wish that I could do it over,
        make some magic move to change it all.
We both crave and covet, mourn and dread,
        the possibility of one more day.

Remembering Frans

When I was beginning to learn, he was the one
who knew everything, or where to find it.
We shared a university library desk,
a goal, a neighborhood, a universe.

We took turns, did not compete for space,
allowed each other's eccentricities.
We blended efforts at the edges, while
our mates, our friends, and others fitted in.

Later we grew—up, apart, then old.
Our separate lives were full—of striving, tensions,
new achievements, accolades—and never
even missed the old shared world. Until

the day I called his wife to share my own
husband's death, and she revealed to me
that hers had lost it all to dementia.
He'll soon remember nothing, not her, not me,

or even the way to the bathroom. This mind
that once filled classrooms, auditoriums,
scholars' journals, books in several tongues,
had turned in upon itself and spun

a web of sticky filaments, capturing
no prey, no food, no victim but itself,
wrapped up in a bundle of wounded thought,
waiting for the tender sting of death.

Bite Me, Death

I've had it up to here with death,
sudden death, lingering death,
lives cut short, plans all thwarted,
futures shattered, dreams aborted,
I'm flat-out tired of your tricks, old sport.

You come too soon, or take too long—
shocking blow for the newly retired,
much too slow for the long demented,
brain tumor blindsides the healthy runner,
lymph cancer violates the sweet young girl.

I've seen all the images of your work—
ironic, histrionic, sardonic, demonic.
Heard all the words that show your style—
stumbled, crumbled, dwindled, declined.
But know that now I'm onto your game.

To lurking ills, to tempted fates:
Do what you will, the future waits.
In the end, I'm sick to death of death.
Your face is clear in the looking glass.
Just know I know you can kiss my ass.

Let in the Light

Lift up the blinds, let in the light:
    the season of death is over,
the season of birth has begun,
    and life will go on.

I planted some seeds long ago,
    in another kind of world.
Two small sprouts flowered freely,
    one white and one red.

The first one bore fruit, while the other
    dropped its blossoms—
nothing seemed to bring its shoots
    any closer to harvest.

I left it to the sun and the rain,
    enjoying its green and occasional red,
thinking, all plants are different. But now
    those red blooms have thrown seeds.

Now the whole landscape has changed:
    the seed of my seed will bear fruit,
the season of death and yearning is done,
    and the season of life is at hand.

New Life Meets Life

Emerging from her cushioned cocoon,
bursting into the world's pain and mess—
a good preview for the lifetime to come—

the babe arrives. She makes no sound,
gives no expression, but her eyes,
already alert, take in the scene.

She attaches her newly separate self
to comforting skins of mother, father,
learns touches and smells that will form her.

As her eyes adjust to life, every day
by ordinary day, she begins to know
faces, voices, that go with the smells.

Not only her vision but all of her being
is opening up, embracing the whole.
So vulnerable, some hurts are in store.

Challenges, changes, surprises of growth
already rise up to shape her future.
She reaches out, arms wide, to grab it all.

Between Two Worlds

Baby in one hand / phone in the other:
Newborn is crying / mother is dying.
I have to be here / I have to be there.

Tiny fingers grip mine tight / large hands calmed my fears.
Here's milk to make her grow / sweet words will help her slow.
Breathing soft, even and strong / breathing soft, fading away.

She's almost asleep / she's almost at peace.
Whispering shhhh / whispering shhhh.
She's letting go / she's letting go.

Butcher Shop Song

The cleaver edge comes ringing down,
once again, out of nowhere,
and a familiar butcher slices off
another indispensable piece of my life.

His white coat is still spattered, smeared,
with blood and fluid from earlier jobs,
and I suspect he moonlights as a medic,
delivering babies to shrieks of pain and joy.

He's decapitated long-time loves and friends,
chopped up others I was just getting to know,
put through his grinder some dear old ones who
had to watch their flesh be processed by inches.

Let him close up shop for a long few years.
He must have enough meat and afterbirth
in storage to last a lifetime, at least until
he readies his cleaver to sing again for me.

All in the Eyes

The son of our daughter, asleep in my arms,
born just a month past your death, wakes up
to see me gazing at him through blurred sight.

As his one-year mark nears, I spy traces of you
in his newly formed face—the quirk of the eyebrows,
the short squared-off chin, quick yell, ready grin.

But it's when I look into his eyes, his eyes,
that I glimpse your own staring out at me, into me
—not at the end, but when we were young—

when he starts to smile: your rebel's bold glance,
when his eyelids droop: your sly bedroom look.
His eyes cleave to mine, and when I smile back,

the knowledge they hold of future and past
floods right back into me, clearing my view,
and once again, at last, I can see.

VI.

Coming Home Alone

Saving Daylight Time

As I stride along the leaf-strewn path,
coming 'round the bouldered curves
along the water's edge, I ponder why

this end of daylight saving time
in fleeting fall makes no more sense
than its beginning. A human stretch

of the natural order, it shocks us
with delight in April but
despair in November.

Why be so greedy for the light
of spring when we will have to pay
the price with autumn's early dusk?

Looking now behind me for your
face amidst the fiery leaves
of these woods at sunset, seeing

only deeper shadows all around,
I feel a certain anger rising up
at how the dark can come so soon.

What Is Life, Anyway?

Sometimes it seems to be a chain of lessons—
alphabet, penmanship, training bra, geometry,
morphing into find God, find career,
find husband, find hiding place.

Or maybe chapters in a storybook, of how
a curious little girl becomes a driven old woman,
subplots packed with drowned uncles,
shooting stars, brides dancing on a beach.

Then again, it's sometimes legal papers,
with sentences linking crimes to punishments,
hasty choices slamming cold iron locks,
mock sacrifices bursting into real flames.

But often it feels more like a ripple of doors
unfolding, not in the path where they should be,
yet opening unexpected gaps in the wall,
alive with teasing glimpses of the blue.

The Other Side of the Leaves

Where the child looks up to see myriad
        veined umbrellas of shade,
the bird gazes on the shiny surfaces
        of each leaf reflecting sun.

Where the deer coming to drink notice
        the lemon cup on the lily pad,
the fish, tilting sideways, peer up
        at parasites swaying on the stem.

Where I look back to find your lifeless
        face, calm, fading by the moment,
perhaps you glance over your shoulder and see
        my hand reaching out to pull you back.

Change of Seasons

Putting away at last my furry, thick,
    enfolding robe of winter,
now changing it for one of lighter weight,
    though still dark-colored and long,
I miss the soothing claustrophobia
    of smothering plush a moment.
It almost seems this thin wrap with no ties
    might let my tender insides
spill out upon the cool hardwood floor,
    so I wonder if it's too soon.
Then again, there is a tickling breeze
    of half-warm air up my sleeves,
as I reach out to get the morning news
    still damp with dawn's fresh drops.

The Riddled Heart

This old pine tree encloses me
with dark meandering branches,
gnarled and bruised like me,
tracing avenues to my past life.

Its boughs spread wide, empty
spaces in between showing
limbs cracked off by heavy winds,
one jagged scar halfway up the trunk
made by some prior lightning strike.

A tentative spring sun warms me
through the maze of twisted twigs,
but darkness still wraps the central
stem that hides its rings within rings,

where the progress of the years
appears to go in circles. Yet
its branch tips burst with growth,
like bristly asterisks trembling
with some eager cryptic message.

New buds make changing patterns
on the half-lit ground below,
wherever the riddled heart
lets the light shine through.

The Return

At my first step out of the door I pause,
breathe in a new layer of warm velvet
riding on the biting breeze beneath.

All the willow boughs are turning yellow,
but a haze of beige still fills winter's view.
Only the evergreens tease the eye with soft

sage-colored puffs between the browns and grays.
Then I hear a whirring, ringing sound above,
look up, searching for some fault in the wires.

Instead it is a cloud of cedar waxwings,
dozens clustered in the oak's bare branches,
tiny beaks thrust up in full-out chirp,

fluffy breasts turned toward the thawing sun.
Next comes the sound of snowmelt trickling fast,
becoming rivulets, rushing into storm drains.

Coming home, my feet hesitate over
perilous frost heaves buckling the pavement;
better to follow the streams along the road.

Ankles aching, I find at last my own pathway,
with water pooling where your boat once sat,
while I soak up that spring can come again.

Nostalgia

Her old friend's surprise visit, forty years overdue,
re-invents her. Once again she's the brave intellectual,
the poet with long hair, long legs, who discovered with him
the cobblestone streets of Europe—and he remembers.

He must of course compare that lithe, long-gone young girl
with this rounded, sagging, far-too-careworn widow
who last night served him apple pie. But does he mourn
the young wife he took to carnival, with her husband away,

on that crazy night they shared so many beers and polkas,
they set the barroom (and her stomach) spinning—when
finally he had to take her home, put her to bed
un-bedded, drawing blankets up, easing doors shut?

Or does he savor the hard-earned warmth and wisdom,
along with the weight and wrinkles, of his old friend,
who for today becomes his expert tour guide as they
now explore the frosty mountains of New England?

Either way, he's brought the young girl back to life.
Her laugh knows that her soul, if remembered, still exists.
And her poet's mind recalls the root of "nostalgia" means
not "fond remembrance" but "pain of longing for home."

A Look in the Mirror

I. Face at Rest

Quiet inside, alone, the face relaxes,
eyes still alert, reflective, recording.
But above them, small collapsed skin-
parachutes drape over the eyelids,
and under, faint bruises show through
where magic coverup has worn off.
Between the brows lurk pillowed creases
where trouble has pressed on too long,
creating this endless look of worry,
while the traitorous mouth persists in
carving downward arcs, determined, or
disappointed at how the years have gone—
which is real, which is masquerade?

II. Face in Play

For show and tell, the forehead smoothes out easily,
fluffs up those wrinkled pillows (an old trick
of tightening the ears). Parachutes inflate,
bruises vanish in newly lifted countenance—
a chain reaction now—as plumping cheeks
draw sullen mouth into fine-tuned curves,
filling tired lips, bending angles back up.
Chin raises, ready now, under-neck snaps
into eager forward thrust, on high alert:
ready to please, introduce, entertain.
This somewhat less-natural state just needs
attention given, a tension paid—why?—
because that's the way the game is played.

Inching On

I look out at distant dimming blue
layers of hills across the lake,
ribbons of mist in powdery dusk,
red sun going down behind them.

Fireball inches toward brooding curves,
and then I see it—small white sailboat
moving ever so slowly across
rippling blue-gray watered silk,

edging its own way toward a brilliant
path the setting sun throws down
from hilltops straight into my eyes.
Somehow it's me in that small sailboat

with its upright mast and slim white jib
crossing shimmering acres of water,
skimming surfaces, sounding depths.
If I do not stop, if I keep inching on,

I could reach that molten pathway
marked out by this eye-piercing sun,
become one with its fierce radiance,
soak up its light, absorb its power.

Small boat sails on past bright mirage,
back to the blue-gray calm, yet now
I too am gilded a moment, ignited
with cataclysmic, life-giving light,

possibly blinded by seeing too much.
So late in the day, so little wind left,
so long yet to go—just keep on going,
inching toward the blue-gray truth.

The Rock at My Back

I find myself the most at peace, at home,
      with a curve of rock behind my back,
      leaning against its steady strength.

Whether jagged from the crackling cold
      or scarred by sudden downhill slides
      or smoothed by weary winds of change,
the rock's rough armor invites my skin,
      responds to my familiar touch,
      tells me about its journey here.

Forged in the heat of the mountain's heart,
      packed solid by the crush of weight,
      thrust up by unknown forces inside,
this rock endured ages of weather extremes,
      until its own proud weight toppled
      its mass down the mountainside.

It found a perch, a nesting place,
      a quiet, cantilevered space,
      to spend the eons, calmer now,
no longer exalted up at the peak,
      but warmed by sun, cooled by mists,
      resting in a more temperate world.

Now it's a pillow of stone for my head,
      a granite cushion for my back,
      a harsh ledge for my fingers' rest.
We are both safe again, for the moment,
      protected against attack from behind,
      positioned to see what's coming ahead.

Seeing Through Trees

A late fall sun peers down through bare trees,
revealing its truth: now you are alone.
With that reality comes a chill
wind of change through their leafless branches,

and mine. I see I am a single tree
standing alone, among others that look
the same but are not connected. Then
it's clear, from the very start I was

but one small growth, trunk straight and true,
running sap with patience, determination,
sending out fresh leaf buds every spring,
expanding by infinitesimal hidden rings.

When I saw you growing nearby, our roots
seemed intertwined: I fed you, you me;
you sheltered me, I you. But since then
you've disappeared, no warning, no farewell.

As your remaining roots die away
underground, mine still thrive, just as
they've done all along. And what's more,
this late fall sun is really early winter.

You're not coming back.
All the trees have lost their leaves.
Now I see the lake.

Do Lilacs Count?

I'm going to steal a moment of your time,
but don't worry, you will get it back. Anyway,
time is only black marks on the clock.

It's true I've committed crimes against your heart,
but you've done the same at my expense.
So maybe we should both be sent to jail.

Or maybe not, because we'd never want
to do the time. Can we just call it even?
It's lucky there are no witnesses but us,

unless the stars keep track of our transgressions.
How many times would the night sky have to turn
before those evening tears become morning dew?

It matters not—if time is only our invention.
I can smell the lilacs waking up right now:
the difference is that lilacs don't count tears.

While I can't make up for all the things we lack,
what I take away I always mean to give back.
Commuting the endless miles into our past,
connecting all the roads, I find only lilacs.

Hidden Wholeness

In the midst of a gray cloud
of swirling talk among us—
audience members waiting
in the crowded concert hall—

the sound of a single cello
cuts a track through verbal fog
with a vibrant silver beam
swelling out deep and wide.

As I turn to follow its path,
the piano's glissando lifts
the dark cloud up and away.
I lean back to breathe in full.

In a pause, more words descend,
like murmuring bees in sunshine
or circling bats in twilight,
urgent, clever, confusing.

Then the piano begins again,
becomes a benign south wind,
joins the cello to blow aside
the buzzing, flapping hum of talk.

It clears the air and brings to light
a new wholeness, always there.
Pure sound lifts our eyes, our hearts,
filling up the empty space between us.

Diving Lessons

Plunge into the stream
of consciousness, amber
river of words tumbling
over ripples and shadows,
slippery dappled rocks—
some are stumbling blocks,
some are crucial shaping forms.

Plummet with a shower
of iridescent fish-thoughts
(glassy eyed, mouths agape)
dangling from the plot-lines,
but don't get hooked,
don't get trapped or caught,
don't stay cornered in the dark.

Plow into the rough and tumble
of the outer rills, trills, thrills;
get some relief by reliving
your loves, laughs, lies;
then sink into the inner life
of rocks and moss and fishes,
as you learn to submerge your self.

Shape what you can, whether
it bends, resists, or breaks.
Take the eons needed
to create a new curve.
Suspend the ache to breathe,
until you can surface again
into the air that awaits you.

Coming Home Alone

If you were waiting with me
to hear the final stanza,
the one with the half-rhyme,

where I enter our empty house alone
and nod to the lake and your ghost
through the back windows,

now is the time for us to let out
that long held breath
and say amen.

In the Palm of My Hand

I. The Promise

You will live long, the gypsy fortune teller said
that magic night when I was seventeen,
as she poked a bony finger at my palm.

Your head line's well-defined, complex. But here,
your heart pathway is crisscrossed in the middle—
shows early passion, then confusion, then

a single groove emerges, clear to the end.
Those fine streaks on your fingers—they mean travel.
Your thumb is strong—perhaps a nurse's life.

Oh, on your wrist I see the three Greek rings
of wealth—you're sure to own two houses, likely
one on water. And that's five dollars please.

II. The Payoff

I'm in good health so far, now two-thirds through
my time—I plan to live at least to ninety—so
who knows? She's been right about a lot:

My head's excelled at learning, problem solving,
helping others reach their goals, their dreams.
And the heart, that old crisscrossed pathway,

almost did me in at mid-life—I wrestled
with right and wrong true things, tangled promises,
and in the end, that line, fading, did not waver.

Travel, for sure, yet painful or unwanted trips
vied with shining voyages. And nurse's thumbs
tended only crumbling parents' lives.

She had her best joke with the three Greek rings:
coins meant not a thing to poets, incoming wealth
slipped through our hands, those houses on the water

more cottages than mansions. Was it worth the five?
Maybe not in outcomes, but perhaps in hopes
still high enough to carry me on, and out.

Epilogue

(In honor of all the poets who inspired me)

How to Use This Drug

They should post warnings on books of poetry—
Do not consume just before bedtime.

Contains: Grains of truth, seeds of dreams,
may cause wakefulness, anticipation,
despair, that results in loss of sleep.

And in fine print: May have elements of
enigmatic words, ambiguous line shifts,
highly saturated syllables,
addictive traces of onomatopoeia.

Caution: Do not exceed maximum dosage,
unless pen and paper are kept at bedside
to catch creative juices flowing from
highly flavored phrases, pungent lines.

Danger: Be prepared to spend remaining
hours of darkness in unaccustomed light—
scribbling, dabbling, quibbling, dribbling—
from exposure to potent language, hidden meanings.

Long-term side effects: Compulsive notation,
loss of daily life, tendency toward isolation,
repetitive behaviors like workshops and readings.

Footnote: If user gets up and turns on
the computer, all hope of sleep is lost.

Acknowledgments

Grateful acknowledgment is made to the editors and publishers of the following journals and anthologies, in which some of these poems first appeared:

Piscataqua Poems: A Seacoast Anthology—"Pulling Anchor," "Ocean Views," "The Surprises of Waves"
The Poets' Guide to New Hampshire 2008—"Old Garden"
The Poets' Guide to New Hampshire 2010—"The Night of Maples Falling"
The Poets' Touchstone—"In the Palm of My Hand," "Seeing Through Trees," "What Is Life, Anyway?" "Almost Open Water," "Traitor"
The Widows' Handbook—"Do You See What I See," "No Answer, No Message"
Wind in the Timothy Press—"Seeing Through Trees"

In addition, I would like to thank North Star Press for accepting *Currents in the Stream*, and their editors and printers for the close attention they have paid to every aspect of publishing this book.

My gratitude goes out to my fellow-poets John-Michael Albert, Barbara Bald, Robert Demaree, and Gordon Lang, who read this manuscript at various stages and made many helpful suggestions. I owe special thanks to Patricia Fargnoli, the former poet laureate of New Hampshire, who first read these poems in their earliest forms, took me seriously as a poet, and encouraged me to go forward in their development.

Lastly, I am grateful to my wonderful family for having faith in my talent, as well as to my late husband Larry, who supported me lovingly, critiqued me fiercely, and thus challenged me to become a better poet than I would have thought possible.

"The highs and lows, the tragedies and comedies, of Charlotte Cox's rich life compress beautifully into the structures of lyric poetry. This is poetry that leaves plenty of room for us, her readers, to fire up our sympathetic memories. It reminds those of us buried in labor-saving technology that a large and vivid life is out there waiting for us, but to reap its rewards we must accept its risks and bravely go out to meet it."

– John-Michael Albert, editor of the 2008 and 2010 *Poets' Guide to New Hampshire*, and Eighth Poet Laureate of Portsmouth, New Hampshire

About the Author

Born in Wisconsin, Charlotte Cox has been writing poetry since she was ten years old. During her school years in the Midwest, her love of words encouraged her to hone skills in fiction, journalism, and literary criticism. Her early working years were spent teaching junior high and high school students to write. Later, she launched a career in the professional world of words with successive jobs as a magazine editor (Illinois), public relations manager (Texas), development administrator (Pennsylvania, North Dakota), and outreach coordinator (Minnesota). However, over the years, less and less of her time was needed for word-crafting, the skill she enjoyed the most.

Finally, in 2004, after forty years of guiding communications devoted to fulfilling the dreams of others, she decided to retire and pursue her own childhood dream of becoming a full-time writer. Upon moving to New Hampshire with her husband, Larry Cox, this vision became possible. Tapping into such vibrant creative writing networks as the New Hampshire Writers Project, Writers in the Round, and the Frost Place Conference on Poetry, she found enough inspiration among the state's many workshops, readings, and circles of fellow writers to launch her new career as a poet.

Since then, Charlotte has won first place in the Poetry Society of New Hampshire's Member Contest, third place in the River Run Seacoast Poetry Contest, and honorable mentions in the PSNH National Contest. Her poems have been published in 2008 and 2010 *Poets' Guide to New Hampshire*, PSNH's *The Poets' Touchstone*, *The Beaver Island Reader*, *Piscataqua Poems: A Seacoast Anthology*, and *The Widows' Handbook* (Kent State University Press, 2014). She has had articles published in *Library Journal, Public Libraries, New Hampshire To Do*, and *Seacoast Living*. She served as the editor of Larry Cox's book, *Close Encounters with the Common Loon* (North Star Press, 2012).

Charlotte has been a featured reader throughout New Hampshire's Lakes Region. In addition, she was invited to read at the Currier Museum's 9/11 Memorial event in Manchester, Wind in the Timothy Press's Poetry Festival in Canterbury, and the Exeter venue of the annual global event called 100 Thousand Poets for Change. She is also an active member of Poets in the Attic in Wolfeboro. Since her husband's death in 2008, Charlotte continues to live in Laconia, sharing her time between developing her writing, supporting her fellow poets, helping out her two daughters' families (one in Henniker, one in Mexico), and enjoying her five grandchildren.